sasol
reaching new fro...

FIRST FIELD GUIDE TO
MAMMALS
OF SOUTHERN AFRICA

SEAN FRASER

Contents

Page 14

Page 44

Mammals

Mammals are animals with a coat of hair or fur which keeps their bodies warm. Unlike birds and reptiles which hatch from eggs, young mammals develop inside their mothers' bodies and are almost fully developed when they are born. After birth they drink milk from their mothers' teats or breasts, until they are able to survive on their own.

Because different mammals live in different environments across the world, and have different habits, their bodies are adapted to the conditions in which they live. Whales have thick layers of fat, called blubber, to keep them warm in cold water; leopards and cheetahs have spots to camouflage them in the long grass when they hunt for prey; and dassies have special pads on their toes to enable them to grip rock surfaces when they climb. Some mammals, such as bats, even have wings so that they can catch their insect prey while they fly.

Page 48

Southern African mammals

Mammals are found on all the continents of the world. Southern Africa has many different mammal species, ranging from the enormous elephant, the biggest land mammal in the world, to the tiny, mouse-like shrew (not featured in this book) – the world's smallest mammal.

Conservation

Because there is such a variety of fascinating mammals in southern Africa, it is important that we help to protect them. Some southern African mammals, such as the zebra-like quagga (*Equus quagga*), are already extinct; others, like the black rhino (*Diceros bicornis*), are endangered, or threatened, and the species could die out entirely if we don't protect it. For this reason, many scientists and researchers study mammals so that we can learn more about them, and through studying them discover how special they are and how we can save them from disappearing altogether.

Page 55

Page 16

Identifying mammals

Page 37

about the way this mammal lives, and so give you some idea as to what species it is. Different animals have different **habits**, and those with which you may not be familiar are marked with a ^G in this book. A definition of these words is given on page 56.

Teach yourself

You can learn about mammals and other animals on your own by teaching yourself:

❀ Join your local library.
❀ Use your school library.
❀ Read magazines on wildlife.
❀ Read stories about animals.
❀ Watch television documentary programmes.
❀ Visit zoos, game reserves, parks.
❀ Go to a natural history museum.
❀ Ask your teacher.
❀ Make your own scrapbook.
❀ Explore the Internet.
❀ Become a member of a conservation organisation or nature group.
❀ Go to special talks and lectures at a local university or college.

In order to identify a specific mammal, you should study its different features, for example, its **size**, **colour**, and **shape**; also, try to see what food it eats, and its surroundings, or **location**. These features may tell you something

Mammal names

Most animals are known by a number of different names. They usually have a **common name**, which is familiar to most of us. But because the same, or similar, animals may have different names in different languages all over the world, most scientists, researchers and conservationists prefer to use the animal's **scientific name**. This is usually a Latin name, and is written in italics. The honey badger, for example, is known by scientists as *Mellivora capensis*.

Sometimes animals are also given different common names by the local people of a specific region. These tribes live in close contact with nature and usually know the different animals of their region well. South African mammals are also known by their Afrikaans (**A**), Xhosa (**X**) or Zulu (**Z**) (the most commonly spoken languages after English) names. For example, the honey badger is also known by its Afrikaans name, ratel, and/or its Zulu name, insele.

Page 47

In the field

Page 20

Most of the mammals that we discuss in this book are only found in the wild, or in game reserves and national parks. But many, for example squirrels, dassies, bats and even whales can be observed in the areas where we live or in the surrounding environment.

Where do I go?
❀ national parks
❀ game and nature reserves
❀ zoos
❀ the beach (whale-watching)
❀ country areas
❀ conservation groups
❀ city walks
❀ your own garden ...

Game-watching
There is a big difference between seeing an animal behind bars in a zoo, and seeing it in its natural environment out in the veld. If you are lucky enough to be able to go game-viewing in one of the country's game reserves, take the time to observe not only the animal you are watching, but also everything around it: the birds,

plants, landscape, and sky – otherwise you may just as well visit the zoo.

In the Kruger National Park, it is best to go game-watching in the dry winter months when most animals visit the watering holes to drink. You will, however, see lots of young mammals there in the summer months. In the Kalahari, game-viewing is best just after the summer rains. If possible, go out into the bush in the morning and late afternoon only, because when it is hot, most animals rest and hide in the shade. They usually only come out to drink and hunt when it is cooler, and it is during these times that you will be able to observe their habits, and see them eating, grooming one another, marking their territory, fighting, and even playing.

What to take

✤ binoculars
✤ a camera or video recorder
✤ a notebook and pen
✤ insect spray
✤ a sun hat and sunscreen
✤ walking shoes or hiking boots
✤ field guides and other books
... but, most importantly, be quiet and keep still ...

Page 12

Egyptian Slit-faced Bat

Nycteris thebaica

African names: Egiptiese spleet-neusvlermuis (A); ilulwane (Z).

Average size: Length 10 cm; wingspan 25 cm; weight 11 g.

Identification: Small; dark, woolly hair covers sturdy body. Long, narrow 'slit' runs down the centre of the face from forehead to nostrils. Ears almost as big as body. Wide wings, rounded at the ends.

Where found: Lives in almost any environment in southern Africa.

Habits: Gregarious[G]; hundreds may roost together in caves, shelters or hollow trees. Nocturnal[G].

Notes: Because bats cannot see very well, the slit in the face has a nose-like function, which enables them to track down prey by using echoes (known as 'echolocation').

Status: Common.

Food: Mostly insects, such as moths and larvae.

Reproduction: Four-month gestation[G]; single offspring weighing 2 g.

Similar species: All other slit-faced bats.

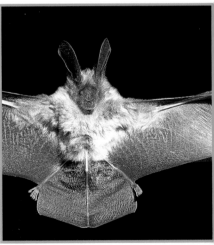

Lesser Bushbaby

Galago moholi

African names: Nagapie (A).

Average size: Length 35 cm; weight 150 g.

Identification: The body is small and covered with a velvety coat. The eyes and ears are big and round. The feet are specially adapted for gripping branches, and the bushy tail is used for balance.

Where found: Savannah woodland, fringes of forests, along rivers, in trees that produce gum.

Habits: Feeds mostly on its own, but sleeps in family groups in nest-like structures made of leaves. Arboreal^G, feeding mostly up in trees; territorial^G. Nocturnal^G.

Notes: Produces a variety of chattering sounds. Some calls resemble a human baby crying.

Status: Common.

Food: Tree gum and resin (especially acacia). It derives necessary water requirements from food; and also berries, insects, and birds' eggs.

Reproduction: Four-month gestation^G; one or two young weighing 9 g each.

Similar species: Thick-tailed bushbaby; Grant's bushbaby.

Chacma Baboon

Papio cynocephalus ursinus

African names: Bobbejaan (A); imfene (X, Z).

Average size: Length 140 cm (m), 110 cm (f); weight 32 kg (m), 15 kg (f).

Identification: Body is relatively large; covered with grey to grey-brown hair. Long, pointed snout. First part of tail is held erect, but rest hangs straight down. Male has powerful shoulders, with a mane around the neck, and a single patch of bare skin under the tail. The female has one patch on each buttock.

Where found: Throughout the region in almost any environment, except in very dry parts.

Habits: Terrestrial[G], but also an excellent climber. Gregarious[G]; troops[G] of 15, or even 100, led by a dominant male. Diurnal[G].

Notes: May try to scavenge from cars. Never feed baboons.

Status: Common.

Food: Omnivorous[G], but mostly fruit, leaves, seeds, grass, roots.

Reproduction: Six-month gestation[G]; single young weighing 800 g.

Similar species: Yellow baboon.

Vervet Monkey

Cercopithecus aethiops

African names:
Blou-aap (A);
inkawu (X, Z).

Average size: Length 110 cm (m),
100 cm (f); weight 6 kg (m),
4 kg (f).

Identification: Body covered in
long, bristly, grey hair; belly is
usually much lighter. Single white
band stretches across forehead
and down sides of cheeks.

Where found: Very adaptable,
but prefers riverine vegetation in
wooded areas and rocky terrain.

Habits: Gregarious^G; troops^G of up
to 20. Good climber, but usually
forages on the ground. Diurnal^G.

Notes: Noisy; produces loud
chattering and scream-like noises
and a distinctive alarm bark to
warn troop^G when a predator is
spotted.

Status: Common.

Food: Mainly fruit, flowers,
leaves and insects.

Reproduction: Five-month
gestation^G; single young
weigh 350 g.

Scrub Hare

Lepus saxatilis

African names: Kolhaas (A); umvundla (X); unogwaja (Z).

Average size: Length 60 cm; weight 3 kg.

Identification: Most noted for its very long ears and powerful hind legs. Coat is soft and fluffy, and dark grey in colour. Tail is small and fuzzy.

Where found: Savannah, woodland and grassland with long grass, bushes and shrubs.

Habits: Usually lives on its own. Nocturnal^G; rests in small hollows in the ground during the day. Moves about by hopping.

Notes: Strong back legs make hares good jumpers and runners. The white undertail is very noticeable when it is on the move. Zimbabwe specimens are smaller.

Status: Common.

Food: Grazes on grass, leaves, and grass roots. Sometimes browses on low bushes.

Reproduction: One to three leverets (young hares) weighing 250 g each are born after a one-and-a-half-month gestation^G period.

Similar species: Cape hare.

Porcupine

Hystrix africaeaustralis

African names: Ystervark (A); ingungubane, inunga (Z).

Average size: Length 90 cm; height 35 cm; weight 18 kg.

Identification: Heavily built creature with a coat of long black-and-white quills extending from the shoulders to the tail. The short, flat tail is covered with white spines. Ridge of softer spines on blunt, rounded head.

Where found: It has very few specific habitat requirements and so is found almost anywhere in the region; usually in burrows[G], caves or crevices in rocks.

Habits: Lives in extended family group with only one breeding pair in each group. Nocturnal[G]; sleeps in holes. Forages along set paths and burrows[G].

Notes: When threatened, it rattles and shakes its quills to scare off enemies; attacks by running backwards (and slightly sideways) to stab attacker with sharp quills.

Status: Common.

Food: Mostly plant matter.

Reproduction: Three-month gestation[G]; one or two young weighing 200 g each.

Similar species: Hedgehog.

Ground Squirrel

Xerus inauris

African names: Waaierstertgrond-eekhoring (A); unomatse (X); ingwejeje, intshidane (Z).

Average size: Length 55 cm; weight 750 g.

Identification: Small, with short, prickly body hair. Usually greyish-brown in colour with a fainter stripe down each side of the body. Small, pointed face with tiny ears. Long, fluffy tail with black and white markings.

Where found: Dry, open areas with little vegetation.

Habits: Highly gregarious^G; large groups of between four and 30 with several dominant females. Diurnal^G; may use bushy tail to shade body from sun. Digs very long burrows^G in which it sleeps. Terrestrial^G.

Notes: Always on the lookout for predators; gives a loud whistle when it senses danger.

Status: Common.

Food: Mostly vegetarian. Diet includes roots, bulbs, grass, pods, and seeds.

Reproduction: One-and-a-half-month gestation^G; two or three young weighing 20 g each.

Similar species: Yellow mongoose.

Brown Hyaena

Hyaena brunnea

African names: Strandwolf, bruinhiëna (A); ingqawane, ingcuka (X); isidawana (Z).

Average size: Length 150 cm; height 80 cm; weight 45 kg.

Identification: High shoulders, sloping back, low rump, all covered with a shaggy, dark brown coat; the mane-like patch of hair around the neck is lighter. Big head with sharply pointed ears. Striped legs.

Where found: Prefers dry areas such as the Kalahari and Namib Desert in Namibia.

Habits: Moves around on its own but shares territory with as many as 10 others. Marks territories with droppings and secretions from anal glands. Nocturnal^G.

Notes: Often stores extra food in special 'pantries'.

Status: Locally common.

Food: Scavenges^G mainly, but may also eat small creatures and even fruit.

Reproduction: Three-month gestation^G; litter^G of two or four cubs weighing 420 g each.

Similar species: Spotted hyaena.

Spotted Hyaena

Crocuta crocuta

African names: Gevlekte hiëna (A); mpisi (X, Z).

Average size: Length 150 cm; height 80 cm; weight 70 kg.

Identification: High shoulders, sloping back, low rump; yellow-brown coat covered with dark splotches; mane-like patch of hair around neck. Big head with large, rounded ears. Short, hairy tail.

Where found: Open plains, woodland savannah and dry areas.

Habits: Usually lives in family groups known as clans, in which females are dominant. Territorial[G]. Marks territories with droppings and secretions from anal glands. Nocturnal[G]. Expert hunter.

Notes: Known as the 'laughing' hyaena; makes human-like chuckling sounds; also shrieks and growls. Its loud 'whoop' call is characteristic of the African night.

Status: Common in protected areas only.

Food: Hunts antelope and zebra but may also scavenge[G].

Reproduction: Three-and-a-half-month gestation[G]; litter[G] of one to two cubs weighing 1,5 kg each.

Similar species: Brown hyaena.

Cheetah

Acinonyx jubatus

African names: Jagluiperd (A); ihlosi (X, Z); ingulule (Z).

Average size: Length 2 m; height 1 m; weight 50 kg.

Identification: The lean body and long legs are pale and covered with black spots from the tail to the head. Black stripes, or 'tears', run down the sides of the face, from the inner eye to the outer corner of the mouth.

Where found: Open spaces and areas with few trees.

Habits: Females live alone with their cubs. Males live alone or in groups of two or three. Hunts during the cooler times of the day by stalking its victim and then making a quick dash for the kill.

Notes: Fastest land animal in the world, reaching about 100 km per hour over short distances.

Status: Locally common.

Food: Feeds on birds, and small- and medium-sized antelope.

Reproduction: Three-month gestation^G; litter^G of three cubs weighing 300 g each.

Similar species: Leopard.

Leopard

Panthera pardus

African names:
Luiperd (A);
ingwe (X, Z).

Average size: Length 190 cm;
height 80 cm; weight 80 kg (m),
50 kg (f).

Identification: Big and strong;
powerful jaws. Body is light-
coloured and covered with small
rosettes[G]. Legs, head and rump
are covered with black spots;
belly is white. Long, rosette[G]-
covered tail is white underneath.

Where found: Able to live almost
anywhere.

Habits: Solitary and territorial[G];
marks territory with droppings
and urine. Nocturnal[G]. Hunts by
stalking, and then leaping out
onto prey.

Notes: Well camouflaged in trees
and tall grasses.

Status: Locally common.

Food: Feeds on birds, antelope,
dassies – and even rats and mice.

Reproduction: Three-and-a-half-
month gestation[G]; one to three cubs
weighing 500 g each.

Similar species: Cheetah.

Lion

Panthera leo

African names: Leeu (A); ingonyama, ibhubesi (X, Z); imbube (Z).

Average size: Length 3 m (m), 2,5 m (f); height 1,5 m (m), 1,2 m (f); weight 200 kg (m), 140 kg (f).

Identification: Largest African predator; light brown to brownish-red in colour; long tail ends in a dark tuft of hair. Male has bushy mane around the head and throat.

Where found: Able to live in almost any habitat.

Habits: Lives in prides[G] of usually two or three males, and several females and their offspring. Females hunt together in groups.

Notes: Lionesses do the hunting, usually at night or towards nightfall, by ambushing prey; males eat first.

Status: Vulnerable.

Food: Hunts most large mammals, including antelope.

Reproduction: Three-and-a-half-month gestation[G]; one to four cubs weighing 1,5 kg each.

Caracal (or Rooikat)

Felis caracal

African names:
Rooikat (A);
ingqawa (X);
indabushe (Z).

Average size: Length 50 cm;
height 90 cm; weight 12 kg.

Identification: Body covered with
soft, red-coloured hair. High rump;
short tail. Very sharp, black-backed
ears with silvery-grey hairs on the
inside and a tuft of black hair on
each tip. White chin, with white
lines under the eyes and nose.

Where found: Able to survive
in almost any habitat, except
for coastal areas.

Habits: Lives on its own.
Nocturnal[G], but may be active
during the day.

Notes: Because it has been
known to attack farm animals such
as sheep and goats, the caracal is
one of the most hunted mammals
in southern Africa.

Status: Rare.

Food: Rodents,
reptiles, ground-
nesting birds, and
small mammals
such as dassies; may
even kill impala and
bushbuck lambs.

Reproduction:
Two-and-a-half-
month gestation[G];
two or three
kittens weighing
250 g each.

African Wild Cat

Felis lybica

African names:
Vaalboskat (A);
imbodla (X, Z);
ingada, ichathaza
(X); impaka (Z).

Average size: Length 90 cm;
height 40 cm; weight 4 kg.

Identification: Body colour
depends on habitat, but is usually
light brown to grey. The throat
and area under the mouth are
usually white, and the underparts,
ears and back legs are red.

Where found:
Prefers to live in
sheltered areas
with long grass
and a few trees
and bushes.

Habits: Usually
lives alone.
Territorial[G];
marks territories
with urine.
Hunts like a
domestic cat.

Notes: Able to crossbreed with
tame, household cats.

Status: SA RDB[G] 'Vulnerable'.

Food: Feeds mostly on rabbits,
mice, rats, snakes, birds, insects
and even spiders.

Reproduction: After a two-
month gestation[G] period, three
or four kittens, weighing 45 g
each, are born.

Similar species: Small-spotted cat.

Bat-eared Fox

Otocyon megalotis

African names: Bakoorjakkals (A).

Average size: Length 90 cm; height 30 cm; weight 4 kg.

Identification: Small, silvery-grey body and black legs. Ears are disproportionately big, compared to small, sharply pointed face; has a grey-white patch over the eyes and nose.

Where found: Occurs fairly commonly in the region, mostly in open scrub grassland.

Habits: Usually lives in pairs or in tight family groups. Mostly nocturnal^G. Digs burrows^G and holes to find food.

Notes: Not a true fox.

Status: Common.

Food: Insects such as harvester termites, and also berries and sometimes small vertebrates.

Reproduction: Two-and-a-half-month gestation^G; litter^G of one to five pups weighing 400 g each.

Similar species: Cape fox.

Wild Dog

Lycaon pictus

African names: Wildehond (A); ixhwili (X); inkentshane, inkontshane (Z).

Average size: Length 130 cm; height 80 cm; weight 25 kg.

Identification: Patches of yellow, white, black and brown hair cover the thin body and long, slender legs. Face is pale, but mouth area is dark; ears are round. Tufted tail is mostly white.

Where found: Savannah woodlands and hilly country; also open plains and areas with short grass and little vegetation.

Habits: Live in packs of about 12; hunt together during early morning or late afternoon. Relentlessly pursue prey; seldom give up until they have made a kill. They only kill to eat. There is only one breeding pair per pack.

Notes: One of Africa's most endangered mammals.

Status: Endangered.

Food: Impala and small antelope.

Reproduction: A two-and-a-half-month gestation[G] period after which a litter[G] of seven to 12 pups weighing 300 g each are born.

Black-backed Jackal

Canis mesomelas

African names: Swartrugjakkals (A); impungutye (X); impungushe, ikhanka, inkanka (Z).

Average size: Length 100 cm; height 45 cm; weight 8 kg.

Identification: Reddish in colour with broad stripe of silvery-black along back, and black tail. Sharp, pointed ears with tufts of white hair inside. Areas around the lower mouth, under the neck and on the chest are almost white.

Where found: Prefers dry areas, but found almost throughout region.

Habits: Usually lives alone, in pairs or in small family packs. Nocturnal[G].

Notes: Known to be very clever, and constantly on the lookout for danger. Wails towards nightfall; also yaps.

Status: Common.

Food: Mice, rabbits, birds, snakes, lizards and fruit, and even small buck. Also carrion[G].

Reproduction: Two-month gestation[G]; litter[G] of one to six pups weighing 380 g each.

Similar species: Side-striped jackal.

Cape Clawless Otter

Aonyx capensis

African names: Groototter (A); intini (X, Z); umthini (Z).

Average size: Length 140 cm; weight 14 kg.

Identification: Long, sleek body with dark coat; white throat and chest. Thick, sturdy legs and strong tail. Finger-like toes rather than obvious claws.

Where found: Found in vegetation along freshwater habitats, as well as in marine areas.

Habits: Lives alone, or female with young. Active at almost any time. Uses fingers to sift through water and silt for food.

Notes: Uses powerful tail and slightly webbed toes to propel body through water;

head is often above the surface. Rough patches under fingers help it to hold onto slippery prey.

Status: Widespread, but nowhere common.

Food: Mostly freshwater crabs and mussels, also frogs and fish.

Reproduction: Two-month gestation[G]; litter[G] of two or three cubs weighing 250 g each.

Similar species: Spotted-necked otter; water mongoose.

Honey Badger

Mellivora capensis

African names:
Ratel (A);
insele (Z).

Average size: Length 95 cm;
height 35 cm; weight 11 kg.

Identification: Thick-set body.
Broad, silvery grey stripe along the
back. Legs are short and tail is
short and bushy. Powerful, sharp
front claws. Strong jaws and teeth.

Where found: Throughout southern
Africa, except in desert regions and
areas with thick vegetation.

Habits: Mainly lives alone.
Nocturnal^G. Aggressive fighter.
Smelly odour is released from
anal glands when stressed.

Notes: Honeyguide bird said to
lead badger to beehives.

Status: SA RDB^G 'Vulnerable'.

Food: Insects, beetle larvae,
reptiles, rodents, birds' eggs
and scorpions.

Reproduction: Six-month
gestation^G; two or three young
weighing 300 g each.

African Civet

Civettictis civetta

African names:
Siwet (A);
inyhwagi (X);
iqaqa (Z).

Average size: Length 130 cm;
height 45 cm; weight 12 kg.

Identification: Body
covered with long, greyish
hair and dark splotches and
stripes. Grey face, with black
bands across eyes and white
muzzle; throat covered with
black-and-white bands. Legs
are long; dark stripe runs
down bushy tail.

Where found: Usually lives in
areas with good vegetation and
a regular supply of water.

Habits: Lives on its own.
Nocturnal[G]. Marks territory
with secretions from anal glands.

Notes: Usually arches its back
while walking. Mane-like ridge
of coarse hair becomes erect when
it senses danger.

Status: Locally common.

Food: Feeds on carrion[G], but
prefers millipedes, insects,
rodents, reptiles, small birds
and wild fruits.

Reproduction: Two-month
gestation[G]; litter[G] of one to
four cubs weighing 100 g each.

Similar species: Tree civet,
small-spotted genet.

Small-spotted Genet

Genetta genetta

African names: Kleinkolmuskeljaat-kat (A); inyhwagi (X); insimba enamabala (Z).

Average size: Length 90 cm; height 25 cm; weight 2,5 kg.

Identification: The body is usually a pale, whitish colour with a grey tint, and is covered with small, dark-coloured spots and blotches. There are white patches around the eyes, the muzzle is dark, and the ears are big and almost transparent. The tail is long and ringed with black bands.

Where found: Able to live almost anywhere in southern Africa.

Habits: Normally solitary. Nocturnal[G], but sometimes seen during the day. Terrestrial[G], but a good climber.

Notes: Musky odour released from scent glands when stressed.

Status: Common.

Food: Feeds mostly on insects, but also takes rats, mice, birds, snakes, lizards, frogs, scorpions, and fruit.

Reproduction: Two-and-a-half-month gestation[G]; three or four young weighing 65 g each.

Similar species: African civet; large-spotted genet.

Suricate

Suricata suricatta

African names: Stokstertmeerkat (A).

Average size: Length 50 cm; height 20 cm; weight 800 g.

Identification: Sharply pointed face, with dark patches around the eyes. Small, lean body of either light brown or light grey; thin tail.

Where found: Dry, open areas.

Habits: Extremely gregarious^G; occurring in groups of between five and 40. Diurnal^G.

Notes: The thin, strong tail is held upright when the suricate runs, but is used for balance when the animal stands up on its back legs.

Status: Locally common.

Food: Mostly insects, but also snakes and lizards.

Reproduction: Two-and-a-half-month gestation^G; three or four young weighing 50 g each.

Similar species: Banded mongoose.

Dwarf Mongoose

Helogale parvula

African names:
Dwergmuishond (A).

Average size: Length 35 cm;
height 15 cm; weight 300 g.

Identification: Small, thin
body covered with a red-brown,
short-haired coat; long, hairy
tail. Pointed face, with small,
rounded ears.

Where found: Open woodlands.
Favours termite mounds for dens,
but will utilize hollow trees or
even deep crevices in rocks.

Habits: Live together in packs,
with a dominant breeding pair.
All pack members help to raise
the young.

Notes: Smallest mongoose. Its
tail is as long as its body.

Status: Common.

Food: Mostly
insects and small
invertebrates, and
sometimes birds
and lizards.

Reproduction:
Two-month
gestation[G]; litter[G]
of one to seven
young weighting
about 20 g each.

Similar species:
Banded mongoose.

African Elephant

Loxodonta africana

African names: Olifant (A); indlovu (X, Z).

Average size: Height 3,4 m (m), 2,5 m (f); weight 6 000 kg (m), 3 500 kg (f).

Identification: World's largest land mammal, grey-brown in colour, with a thick, leathery skin. Trunk 1,5 m long; big ears, tusks.

Where found: Dry savannah and woodland. Needs plenty of food and water.

Habits: Small family groups of mothers and calves led by an old cow. Bulls live separately in small groups.

Notes: Usually not dangerous, but will charge if wounded or when protecting calves.

Status: Common.

Food: Eats about 300 kg of plants, fruits, leaves and grass, and drinks about 200 litres of water in a day.

Reproduction: 22-month gestation^G; single calf weighing 120 kg. Only breed every three to four years.

Rock Hyrax (or Dassie)

Procavia capensis

African names:
Klipdassie (A);
imbila (X, Z).

Average size: Length 50 cm;
height 30 cm; weight 3,5 kg.

Identification: Small, stocky
body covered with light to dark
brown hair; no tail. Sharply
pointed face; small, rounded ears.
Short legs; glands on feet secrete
moisture which enables animal
to grip rock surfaces.

Where found: Rocky,
mountainous terrain.

Habits: Lives in groups of
up to 17 females together
with their young, with a single
dominant male. Diurnal[G], but
may feed at night.

Notes: One adult keeps guard
while others feed or lie in the
sun; gives a warning call when
sees or hears danger, so that group
can take cover (usually nearby).

Status: Common.

Food: Leaves, fruit
and grass.

Reproduction:
Seven-month
gestation[G]; two
or three young
weighing 200 g
each.

Similar species:
Tree dassie, yellow-
spotted rock dassie.

White Rhinoceros

Ceratotherium simum

Vulnerable to poaching: population distribution confidential.

African names: Witrenoster (A); umkhombe (X); ubhejane, omhlophe (Z).

Average size: Height 1,8 m; weight 1 800 kg.

Identification: Lips are square-shaped. Has two horns, and big, pointed ears. Prominent hump on the back of the neck.

Where found: Lots of short grass, shady bushes and fresh water.

Habits: Lives in groups of three or four; males territorial[G]. Poor eyesight, but quick to respond to dangerous sounds or smells.

Notes: Because it regularly rolls in the dust, it appears sand-coloured. A rhino's horns are made of a hair-like fibre, not of bone or ivory.

Status: Vulnerable.

Food: Grazer[G]; feeds on short grasses and low-growing plants.

Reproduction: 16-month gestation[G]; single calf of 40 kg.

Similar species: Black rhinoceros.

Black Rhinoceros

Diceros bicornis

Highly endangered: population distribution confidential.

African names: Swartrenoster (A); umkhombe (X); ubhejane, isibhejane (Z).

Average size: Height 1,5 m; weight 900 kg.

Identification: Greyish brown in colour with thick skin. Two horns and short tail. Pointed upper lip hooks over the bottom lip. Head is smaller than white rhino's.

Notes: Drops its dung in special areas called middens or latrines[G]. Searches for food when it is cool.

Status: SA RDB[G] 'Endangered'.

Food: Browser[G]. Uses its pointed upper lip to pull leaves and twigs from shrubs.

Reproduction: 15-month gestation[G]; single calf weighing 40 kg.

Similar species: White rhinoceros

Where found: From deserts to areas with shrubs and trees that give plenty of shade.

Habits: Lives alone. Has poor eyesight, but a keen sense of smell.

Burchell's Zebra

Equus burchellii

African names: Bontsebra (A); dube (X, Z).

Average Size: Height 1,3 m; weight 300 kg.

Identification: White body covered all over with black stripes, but southern African species has brownish shadow-like stripes too, especially on the rump. Long mane of black-and-white hair which stands upright.

Where found: Open grassland and savannah plains.

Habits: Lives in small family groups, but may also be seen grazing with antelope such as wildebeest.

Notes: Young males may form bachelor^G herds. Stallions are fiercely protective of their mares.

Status: Common in protected areas.

Food: Grazes^G on grasses, but may also browse^G on leaves and shoots.

Reproduction: 12-month gestation^G; single foal weighing 30 kg.

Similar species: Cape mountain zebra.

Warthog

Phacochoerus aethiopicus

African names: Vlakvark (A); ingulube (X); indlovudawana intibane (Z).

Average size: Height 70 cm (m), 60 cm (f); weight 80 kg (m), 60 kg (f).

Identification: Powerful body and pig-like face with long snout. Pronounced bumps ('warts') above nostrils and on either side of eyes. Grey skin covered with scattered bristly hair. Long-haired mane; very thin tail ending in clump of hair. Adults have curved tusks, and whisker-like hairs on the sides of the face.

Where found: Prefers wide, open woodlands.

Habits: Family groups (called 'sounders') consist of a mother and her litter^G, sometimes a boar; boars usually in bachelor^G herds. Diurnal^G.

Notes: Tail held upright when running. Kneels on front legs when feeding. Uses tusks (two pairs), which are actually canine teeth, as weapons.

Status: Common.

Food: Mostly grazers^G, feeding on grass and plant roots.

Reproduction: Six-month gestation^G; two or three piglets weighing 600 g each.

Similar species: Bushpig.

Hippopotamus

Hippopotamus amphibius

African names:
Seekoei (A);
imvubu (X, Z).

Average size: Height 1,5 m;
weight 1 500 kg.

Identification: Huge body covered
in smooth, dark-grey skin.
Massive, powerful jaws; huge
canine and incisor teeth. Short
legs, with four toes on each foot.

Where found: Rivers, lakes
and lagoons.

Notes: Can hold breath under
water for five or six minutes.
Nostrils close automatically
when the head is under water.
Body produces red-coloured
liquid to keep skin moist.

Status: Locally common.

Food: Grazer^G; feeds mostly on
grass and small plants on or near
river banks and lagoons.

Reproduction: Mates in the water;
single calf weighing 30 kg born
after eight-month gestation^G period.

Habits: Lives
in groups
of about 12
cows and
calves headed
by a bull.
Roams river
banks at
night. Bulls
mark their
territory by
spreading
their dung.

Giraffe

Giraffa camelopardalis

African names: Kameelperd (A); indlulamthi, icowa, umcheya (X); indlulamithi (Z).

Average size: Height 4,5 m (m), 4 m (f); weight 1 200 kg (m), 900 kg (f).

Identification: Tall; long, thin legs and long, sturdy neck. Coat covered with mottled brown patches. Sharp, pointed face; two horn-like knobs (covered with skin) on the head.

Where found: Thornveld.

Habits: Lives in groups of up to 20; most active in early morning and late afternoon.

Notes: Makes snorting sounds. It is the tallest land mammal.

Status: Locally common.

Food: Browser^G; spends three quarters of day eating from high branches. Curls its lips and 45-cm tongue around twigs and pulls off leaves. Favours acacia trees.

Reproduction: 15-month gestation^G; single calf weighing 100 kg.

Blue Wildebeest

Connochaetes taurinus

African names: Blouwildebees (A); Nkhonhoni (X, Z).

Average size: Height 1,5 m (m), 1,3 (f); weight 250 kg (m), 180 kg (f).

Identification: Dark grey body, with broad chest and wide shoulders. Stripe-like marks running down from neck to chest. Broad face with hair hanging from the throat; pair of curved horns; long-haired tail.

Where found: Open savannah and plains covered with grass.

Habits: Gregarious^G. Usually herds of up to 30, but sometimes thousands when migrating^G. Bulls are strictly territorial^G.

Notes: Calves can walk almost immediately after they are born. Its horns are not as curved as black wildebeest's.

Status: Common.

Food: Grazes^G on short grasses.

Reproduction: Eight-month gestation^G; single calf weighing 20 kg.

Similar species: Black wildebeest.

Blesbok

Damaliscus dorcas phillipsi

African names:
Blesbok (A).

Average size: Height 90 cm; weight 70 kg.

Identification: Strong chest and low rump covered with a short-haired coat of red-brown; saddle and underparts lighter. Long, white muzzle, and pointed white ears. Both sexes have ridged, outward-curving horns.

Where found:
Prefers wide, open grassy plains.

Habits: Form herds; bulls are strictly territorial[G]. When frightened, they flee in a long line. Create their own middens[G].

Notes: Both males and females have horns.

Status: Common.

Food: Exclusively a grazer[G].

Reproduction: Eight-month gestation[G]; single lamb weighing 6 kg.

Similar species: Bontebok.

Common Duiker

Sylvicapra grimmia

African names: Grys duiker, gewone duiker (A); mpunzi (X, Z).

Average size: Height 60 cm; weight 18 kg.

Identification: Small body with grey- to dark-brown coat of short hair, and long, thin legs. Tuft of long hair on top of the head; may have a stripe of dark hair on the snout. Rams have sharply pointed horns.

Where found: Commonly found in most areas, but prefers bushy terrain and wooded savannah.

Habits: Usually lives on its own, but sometimes seen in pairs. Territorial^G. Diurnal^G in wilderness regions.

Notes: Small glands on inner eyes secrete a substance which is rubbed off on twigs and grass stems to mark territories.

Status: Abundant.

Food: Browses^G on shoots, leaves, flowers, fruit, and sometimes farm crops. Has also been known to eat insects, and even carrion^G.

Reproduction: Six-month gestation^G; single lamb weighing 1,5 kg.

Similar species: Blue duiker, red duiker, oribi, klipspringer.

Springbok

Antidorcas marsupialis

African names: Springbok (A); ibhadi (X); insephe (Z).

Average size: Height 75 cm; weight 40 kg.

Identification: Small body; light-brown back, white belly, and broad, dark red-brown stripe on the sides. Thin, strong legs, and long, pointed ears. Both ram and ewe have curved, ridged horns, but the male's horns are thicker. Tiny tail.

Where found: Dry, open areas with little vegetation.

Habits: Usually form small herds, but may come together in thousands, especially during migration[G].

Notes: When frightened, the springbok 'pronks', leaping straight-legged into the air with back arched.

Status: Common.

Food: Largely a grazer[G], but may also browse[G].

Reproduction: Five-and-a-half-month gestation[G]; single lamb weighing 3,5 kg.

Klipspringer

Oreotragus oreotragus

African names:
Klipspringer (A);
liza (X); igogo (Z).

Average size: Height 60 cm;
weight 12 kg.

Identification: Fairly small
antelope with rough, bristly
coat. Body greyish in colour,
but belly and lower face almost
white. Short, rounded ears, and
bead-like eyes. Only male has
short, pointed horns.

Where found: Only in very
rocky areas.

Habits: Live in pairs with most
recent offspring.

Notes: Only antelope that walks
on the tips of its small hooves.
Special glands located under the
eyes give off a secretion which
is used to mark territory on twigs
and branches.

Status: Common.

Food: Usually browses^G, but
sometimes eats grasses.

Reproduction: Seven-month
gestation^G; single lamb weighing
1 kg.

Steenbok

Raphicerus campestris

African names: Steenbok (A); shabanga (X); qhina (Z).

Average size: Height 50 cm; weight 13 kg.

Identification: Small, graceful body covered with light-brown coat; white on the belly. Small head with white patch on the neck and around the eyes; large ears. Rams have short, sharply pointed horns.

Where found: Usually in open grasslands with some trees and rocks for shelter.

Habits: Usually lives on its own, but a pair share a territory which they defend. May be active during day and night. Creates its own middens^G, which are lightly covered with soil.

Notes: Runs very fast in zig-zag pattern as it flees, and may stop to look back.

Status: Abundant.

Food: Mainly browses^G on young leaves, shoots, flowers and fruit. May also dig for roots with their hooves.

Reproduction: Six-month gestation^G; single lamb weighing 900 g.

Similar species: Sharpe's grysbok, oribi.

Impala

Aepyceros melampus

African names:
Rooibok (A);
impala (X, Z).

Average size: Height 90 cm;
weight 50 kg.

Identification: Medium-sized,
with a red-coloured back, slightly
lighter sides, and white underparts.
Only rams have the outward-
curving horns.

Where found: Open woodland
areas with some cover from
predators (bushes and small trees).

Habits: Rams live in bachelor[G]
herds; females form herds during
the mating season. Diurnal[G].

Notes: Has gland above hoof on
each hind leg for marking territory.

Status: Common.

Food: Grazer[G].

Reproduction: Seven-and-a-half-
month gestation[G]; single lamb
weighing 5 kg.

Similar species: Black-faced
impala.

Gemsbok (or Oryx)

Oryx gazella

African names: Gemsbok (A); inkukhama (X).

Average size: Height 1,2 m; weight 220 kg.

Identification: Solid body; greyish in colour, with clear black-and-white marks on face, upper legs, rump and lower body. A broad black stripe runs down the throat. Thick neck. Tail of long dark hair. Both male and female have long, straight horns.

Where found: Prefers dry grassland and desert dunes.

Habits: Herds of about 15, consisting of bulls, cows and calves or only cows and calves. Bulls territorial[G].

Notes: To prevent the gemsbok's brain from overheating, blood passes through a special cooling system in the animal's nose, and once it has cooled down, flows on to the brain.

Status: Locally common.

Food: Eats mostly dry grass or shrubs; also wild melons for moisture content. Can survive mostly without water.

Reproduction: Nine-month gestation[G]; single calf weighing 15 kg.

African Buffalo

Syncerus caffer

African names:
Buffel (A);
inyathi (X, Z).

Average size: Height 1,4 m;
weight 700 kg.

Identification: Sturdy, dark-brown body; wide, strong back; short legs and large hooves. Ears are long and hang below the face. Tuft of dark hair on tip of tail. Males and females have massive, curved horns.

Where found: Prefers woodland savannah.

Habits: Gregarious[G]; lives in herds which can include hundreds of animals – males, females and their young. Some bulls may form small bachelor[G] herds.

Notes: Although both cows and bulls have big horns, the bull usually has a much heavier 'boss', or hard, cap-like base of the horn.

Status: Locally common.

Food: Grazer[G].

Reproduction: 11-month gestation[G]; single calf weighing 40 kg.

Kudu

Tragelaphus strepsiceros

African names: Koedoe (A); iqudu (X); umgankla, igogo, igoqo, imbodwane (Z).

Average size: Height 150 cm; weight 250 kg (m), 180 kg (f).

Identification: Light brown body, with pale stripes running down each side. Large, leaf-shaped ears, and a bushy tail. The bull has impressive spiral horns.

Where found: Lives in savannah woodland areas, and even dry, rocky landscapes.

Habits: Cows and calves form herds of about four to 10, while bulls live either on their own or in bachelor^G herds. Diurnal^G.

Notes: Excellent jumpers, reaching heights of over 2 m!

Status: Common.

Food: Browser^G; eats the leaves of an enormous variety of different bushes and low trees – more than any other antelope in southern Africa.

Reproduction: Seven-month gestation^G; single calf weighing 15 kg.

Eland

Taurotragus oryx

African names:
Eland (A);
impofu (X, Z).

Average size: Height 1,7 m (m),
1,5 m (f); weight 750 kg (m),
450 kg (f).

Identification: Huge; cow-like
body. Dark mane running down the
neck; long tail which ends in
a clump of dark hair. Both bull
and cow have horns which are
slightly twisted.

Where found:
Savannah
woodland and
dry plains.

Habits: Herds
of 20 to 60, but
sometimes herds
may come
together for short
periods to form
large groups
of more than
1 000 animals.

Notes: Can survive without
drinking water, relying on wild
cucumbers and melons for
moisture intake.

Status: Locally common.

Food: Browses^G, but also
digs for roots. Can go for long
periods without water.

Reproduction: Nine-month
gestation^G; single calf weighing
30 kg.

Waterbuck

Kobus ellipsiprymnus

African names:
Waterbok (A);
phiva (Z).

Average size: Height 1,2 m;
weight 220 kg.

Identification: Well-built body
with shaggy greyish or brown coat.
Males have long, ridged horns
which curve upwards. Distinct
white ring around the rump area.

Where found: Almost always
near water; prefers dense,
woody vegetation with
tall grass.

Habits: Gregarious^G. Small
herds of about 10, with one
adult bull. Young bulls may
form bachelor^G herds.

Notes: Bulls are strictly
territorial^G, especially
during mating season.

Status: Common.

Food: Grazes^G mainly on
grasses, but may also
browse^G.

Reproduction: Nine-
month gestation^G; single
calf weighing 13 kg.

Common Dolphin

Delphinus delphis

African names: Gewone dolfyn (A) ihlengesi (X); ihlengethwa (Z).

Average size: Length 2,5 m; weight: 150 kg.

Identification: Dark grey back, with grey and mustard-coloured shapes on the sides; dark stripe from around the eyes down into long beak. Sharp, curved dorsal fin; long, tapered pectoral fins.

Where found: Shallow and deep, warm pelagic (sea) waters throughout the region.

Habits: Commonly found in groups of about 20. Dives underwater for only short periods. Jumps out of the water when chasing flying fish.

Notes: Curved criss-cross pattern along its sides.

Food: Small fish, such as anchovies and sardines, and squid.

Reproduction: 11-month gestation[G]; single calf is one-metre-long and weighs 40 kg.

Status: Common offshore.

Similar species: Bottlenose dolphin.

Southern Right Whale

Eubalaena australis

African names: Suidelike noordkaper (A); umkhoma (Z).

Average size: Length 17 m; weight 60 t.

Identification: Very large, dark grey body, with heavy front tapering towards the large pointed flukes (at end of tail). Pectoral fins shaped like a paddle; no dorsal fin. Whale lice and barnacles settle on areas of thick skin (callosites) on head – making them white.

Where found: Migrates[G] between waters of the Antarctic (November to April), and oceans north and south of the tropics (May to October).

Habits: Swims slowly. Whales 'breach', or push their bodies backwards out of the sea, then crash back down into the water.

Notes: Called southern 'right' whale because was considered by early whalers as the 'right' whale to hunt, because it floats when dead.

Status: Seasonally common.

Food: Specialist feeder on copepods[G].

Reproduction: 12-month gestation[G]; single calf measuring 6 m.

Cape Fur Seal

Arctocephalus pusillus

African names: Kaapse pelsrob (A); intini yaselwandle (X); imvu yamanzi (Z).

Average size: Length 220 cm (m), 160 cm (f); weight 250 kg (m), 75 kg (f).

Identification: Torpedo-shaped body covered in dark brown, almost black hair. Males are especially dark, with mane-like hair around the throat and neck. Four flippers. Whiskers on side of pointed face.

Where found: Coastal land and water.

Habits: Live in colonies of hundreds when breeding. Adult bulls mark out territories at breeding spots.

Notes: About seven days after giving birth to her pup, the mother returns to sea to hunt. On return, she calls for her pup who recognises her immediately by her call.

Status: Locally common.

Food: Prefers fish that swim in large schools, such as pilchards and sardines.

Reproduction: Gestation^G approximately 12 months; single offspring weighing 3 kg.

Similar species: Other seal species.

Glossary

Arboreal: Living in trees.
Bachelor: Non-breeding male.
Browser: An animal that feeds on the leaves and fruits of trees and bushes.
Burrow: A tunnel or hole dug in the ground to offer shelter.
Carrion: Dead and rotting meat.
Copepods: One of the many micro-organisms that make up plankton.
Diurnal: Active during the day.
Fynbos: Numerous species of narrow-leaved shrubs common to winter rainfall areas such as the Western Cape.
Gestation: Pregnancy; time during which developing young is carried in the womb of the mother.
Grazer: An animal that feeds mostly on grass and ground-covering plants.
Gregarious: Social; living in groups or colonies.
Latrine or Midden: The area where droppings are deposited; 'toilet'.
Litter: A group of young animals produced at one birth.

Migrating/migrant: Moving from one region to another, with the seasons.
Nocturnal: Active at night.
Omnivore: An animal that eats both meat and plants.
Pride: A group of three to 20 lions, but may include up to 30 lions.
Rosette: A small group of spots on the leopard's coat.
SA RDB: South African Red Data Book listing rare and endangered species.
Scavenger: An animal that feeds on the carcass of an animal it did not kill itself.
Terrestrial: Living on the ground.
Territorial: Staying in a marked off area, which is defended against others.
Troop: A group of monkeys or baboons.

Photographic Credits

Nigel Dennis: front cover (bottom right), pg 1, 3, 4, 6 (SIL), 8, 12, 13, 15, 17, 18 (SIL), 19, 20, 21, 22, 23, 24 (SIL), 25, 26, 29, 30, 31, 32 (SIL), 33, 35, 36, 37, 38, 39, 40, 42 (SIL), 47, 48, 49, 51, 52 (SIL), 55, 56, back cover; **Wendy Dennis:** pg 5; **R. Haestier:** pg 53; **Lex Hes:** pg 28, 50; **Leonard Hoffmann/SIL:** pg 2, 14; **Peter Pickford:** pg 41, 43 (SIL), 54 (SIL); **Austin J. Stevens:** pg 5, 7, 9, 12, 16, 27, 44, 45; **Erhardt Thiel/SIL:** pg 34; **Lanz van Horsten/SIL:** front cover (top, left, centre), pg 46; **John Visser:** pg 10, 11; **David Thorpe/SIL:** pg 54 (illustration).
SIL = Struik Image Library

Page 13